Sharing JESUS

Kathleen Cortright

Print information available on the last page

Rev. date: 12/05/2018

To order additional copies of this book, contact:
Xlibris
1-888-795-4274
www.Xlibris.com
Orders@Xlibris.com

Dedication

This little book tells how Kathleen shares Jesus through the Bible scriptures, all the while learning herself. She enjoys telling everyone about Jesus and His love.

I want to dedicate this book to my family. Without them, who knows where I would be?

To my husband, Ernie, thank you for taking me to church from the beginning of our relationship. You told me that if our friendship was going anywhere, we must go to church.

To my kids, David, Misty and Bill. You have given me a reason to go on. We are a blended family of his kids and mine. I am so thankful that God made it possible to love and care for each other. If God is for us, who can be against us?

A special thank you to Misty. As Ernie and I have aged, she has sacrificed her life to care for us. It has allowed for us to stay in our home.

To my grandkids, Jordan, Elly, William, Liam, and Ari. I love you. I pray that you know and love Jesus.

Hebrews 13:5

Kathleen was a very bright 10-year-old girl. She lived with her mom and dad and her brother, Clifford. But she called him Cliffy. He was 4 years older.

Kathleen loved Jesus. She met Him at church in her Sunday School class when she was 6. Mr. Garrett, her teacher told her all about Him and how much He loved her. He gave His life as payment for our sins. He saved us from eternal death.

When Kathleen prayed, she could feel Jesus holding her in His arms. It was always a warm, good feeling. Before she went to sleep, she would kneel beside her bed and pray. "God bless Mommy and Daddy and Cliffy and me."

But tonight, she couldn't feel Jesus wrap His loving arms around her. This made her very sad. "Where is He?" she wondered.

She stood up to go look for Him. He wasn't in her room, at least that's what she thought. She went into Cliffy's room, but no one was there. Not even Cliffy. He wasn't in the kitchen.

"Where could He be? I hope He hasn't left me."

"Jesus! Jesus!" She cried as she walked around the house. She was getting very worried as tears were rolling down her cheeks. Could He even hear her?

She went back to her room and crawled into bed. As she lay there, she closed her eyes. Then, in her mind's eye, she could see Him. He said to her, "Kathleen, I hear you when you pray. I know your needs and I will provide. I will never leave you nor forsake you. I am always near."

In the morning, she told her mother what had happened last night.

"Kathleen, sometimes Jesus likes to play hide and go seek. He wants you to seek Him with all of your heart and with eagerness."

He promises us in Hebrews 13:5, "I will never leave you nor forsake you." Everything we need to know about Jesus is in the Bible.

Let's pray, "Jesus help us to know you are always near and that you are always by our side encouraging us. Talk to us through Your Holy Word. Let us always keep our mind on You. Amen."

Hebrews 13:16

Kathleen was so excited. Today, her best friend, Pam was coming over for a playdate. She had known Pam all her life. Their mothers were best friends, so they were together quite often.

Kathleen's birthday had brought her all kinds of toys. Her favorite was a box of paper projects. Today, they were going to make greeting cards.

The doorbell rang. Kathleen ran to the door. "She's here!" Kathleen squealed.

Her mom set up a table in her bedroom. There would be plenty of room to spread out the contents. The girls were eager to get started.

As they pawed through the box, there was a strange feeling in Kathleen's stomach. She just didn't want to share all this. She didn't want Pam to use her scissors or her paper, or her glue. She selfishly wanted it all herself.

She grabbed the scissors to put back into the box. She picked it all up as Pam stared in disbelief. What was her best friend doing? She had never known Kathleen to be selfish.

Kathleen's mother walked into the room to see what the noise was about just as Kathleen slapped the box shut. She got up and put the box in her closet. She returned to her chair, sat down and crossed her arms over her chest.

"Kathleen Laura!!" Her mom said sternly. "What are you doing?"

"I don't want anyone to use my stuff."

"God is not pleased with your selfishness," her mother remarked. It says clearly in Hebrews 13:16,

"But do not forget to do good and to share for with such, God is well pleased."

That wasn't what Kathleen wanted to hear. Kathleen could feel her Precious Jesus tugging at her heart. She didn't want to make Him upset with her. She decided to listen to what Jesus wanted her to do. She got up to retrieve the box and share with Pam. It felt good to be obedient.

I Chronicles 16:34

It was Sunday and Mr. Garrett was telling his Sunday school class about mercy, God's mercy. "God's mercy endures forever and He is quick to forgive us if we ask with sincerity. It's when God gives us a second chance to do the right thing."

I Chronicles 16:34, tells us "Give thanks to the Lord for He is good and His mercy endures forever."

On Monday, Kathleen, Misty and Pam were in the back seat of the SUV. They were headed to the Raley's supermarket so mom could do some grocery shopping. That would be boring.

Mom promised that if the girls were good and didn't argue, they would stop for an ice cream.

No sooner had they climbed into the back seat, when they were already arguing about ice cream flavors.

"Chocolate is the best!" blurted Kathleen!

"No way!" said Misty. "Pistachio is the very best. It's my favorite!"

Pam, not to be outdone said, "You're both wrong! The best is chocolate with peanut butter, I might get 2 scoops, with chocolate syrup and whipped cream!"

Kathleen's mom turned around, gave the girls a glare and said," Girls! If you don't quit that bickering, we'll skip the ice cream shop completely."

"But mom" whined Kathleen, "even God gives us forgiveness from our faults."

"Kathleen, are you asking for mercy?"

"I guess I am. We are sorry for not minding you. It's better when we don't argue,"

If we repent of our sins and ask forgiveness. God will give us mercy so we can restore our relationship with Him!"

John 3:17

Kathleen squirmed in her pew seat. She was waiting for church to start. She usually went to children's church in the morning. But today she got to go to the adult service. She saw a homeless man sitting in the second pew. He was grubby and needed a shave and a haircut.

She heard Mrs. Springer say, "That man should be kicked out of here. He clearly doesn't belong." Kathleen felt sorry for him. He looked so lost and alone. "Who does belong here?" she asked herself.

Didn't Jesus come to Earth to save the lost? God sent His Son, Jesus into this world that through Him the world would be saved. John 3:17

Kathleen was thinking that most people think that Jesus is the punisher. If you sin, He is here to condemn you to death. But that's not the truth. By believing in Jesus as our Savior, we can have life forever.

Kathleen wanted to tell the homeless man this. Should she go to him? What if he got mad at her? Oh well, she would put on her cutest smile. Who could resist this face?

As she walked up to him, he smiled, "Yeah, this is going to work." she thought. She began to tell him about a man named Jesus. He was actually listening to her! "Do you want to get forgiveness from Jesus and ask Him to come into your heart?" She looked up into his eyes and saw that he was tearing up.

"Yes! Yes, I do!" he replied. "Would you show me how?"

"I would love to introduce you to Jesus," she told him.

She led him in prayer. Just as he was finishing, Mrs. Springer walked up to him to ask him to leave.

Kathleen stopped her in midsentence to tell her that Mr. George was now a brother in the Lord.

You could sure see a difference in Mr. George's face. He was smiling with a huge grin. Mrs. Springer took a step backward with a surprised look on her face. "Welcome to the family of God!" she whispered.

Matthew 25:40

Kathleen awoke very early this morning. It was Saturday and she was going with her mom to "feed the hungry" downtown. She had never done that before and was curious to see how it worked. Her mom had been going for several years and decided that Kathleen was ready to help.

Kathleen had wonderful loving parents. Her dad made good money to support the family. There was always good food on the table so she didn't know what it felt like to be really hungry. Her mom was an attractive stay-at-home mom. Kathleen loved that her mom was always there for her.

Kathleen couldn't imagine going hungry, it had never happened to her. Others were less fortunate. Her mom told Kathleen that Jesus said we should feed the hungry. When we feed the poor and hungry, it's like we are feeding Jesus. He said in Matthew 25:40, "If you do it for the least person, you are doing it for me."

When Kathleen saw all the hungry people waiting for food, she was surprised and a bit frightened. They didn't look or dress like her friends and family. It didn't take long for Kathleen to warm up to them though, she always made friends easily.

Kathleen's job was to hand out sandwiches. There was peanut butter and jelly for the kids. As she gave a sandwich to each child, she told them, "Jesus loves you!"

"Who is Jesus?", little ten-year-old Marcie asked. Kathleen told Marcie all about the Savior and how much He loved children. Marcie gobbled the sandwich down eagerly. "Mmmm, so good, tell me more about Jesus, Kathleen", said Marcie. They became friends!

This is what Kathleen told Marcie:

God sent his only Son Jesus to Earth to save the people and to show his people how to live. If you ask Jesus to forgive you of your sins and invite him to live in your heart, he will forgive you. You must ask him sincerely and then not sin again.

John 14:1-14

Kathleen was combing her doll's hair when her brother, Cliffy came into her room. He rarely came into Kathleen's room. He had a strict rule that she was not to go into his room.

"Older brothers are mean. He won't let me play with his cars." But she always messed with his stuff and he didn't like that.

So, she was surprised when he came into her room.

"Did you know that Jesus made reservations for us in heaven?" he asked.

"What do you mean we have reservations in heaven?"

"It says in the Bible, John 14:1-14 that His Father's house has many rooms in it. Jesus has gone to set up our rooms in God's house. Then, He is coming back for us and take us to His Father's house." Jesus told His disciples there He had prepared a place for us.

One of the disciples asked what was the way to His Father's house. He answered, "You know the way....I am the Way, the Truth and the Life. No man comes to the Father except through Me."

"Wow! Cliffy, now we know where we are going and where we will live. In God's House!"

I Peter 5:7 Matthew 6:25-33

Wanda was obviously very worried about something. She was wiggling around in her chair and sighing deeply. Sunday school was about to start. Mr. Garrett walked into class and noticed right away that Wanda was upset.

"What's the matter, Wanda? You look concerned about something."

"My brother was in a bad motorcycle accident. He had a head injury and is recovering slowly. He's missed a lot of work and can't afford to pay his bills."

"The Bible says, in I Peter 5:7 "Cast all your cares on Jesus because He cares for you," said Mr. Garrett. "No problem is too small for God and nothing is too big. We can take any of our cares to him. He hears you and knows the best plan for your life. I'm sure God will take care of your brother, Wanda, if we pray firm in our faith."

"Kathleen, will you pray with me?"

"Sure, Wanda, I like to pray."

"I don't know any fancy prayers, Kathleen. How do I talk to Jesus?"

"Just talk to him like you would talk to me. He doesn't expect fancy words from us. Just say, "Hello Jesus, I need to talk to you about my brother. He is hurt very badly and needs a healing from you. I pray that You would touch him now. I pray in your holy name."

It's very simple. God is very glad when we pray.

So, cast your burdens unto Jesus, He cares for you.

God tells us that it's a sin to worry. We are not supposed to worry.

Matthew 6:25 tells us, "Do not worry about your life..."

6:27: Which of you, by worrying can add one cubit to his stature?

6:28: Why do you worry about clothing?

6:31: Do not worry saying, "What shall we eat? What shall we drink? What shall we wear?"

6:33: But seek first the kingdom of God and His righteousness and all these things shall be added unto you.

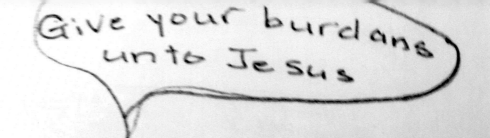

Matthew 16:5-15

"Mom?" Kathleen asked, "What is a prayer closet? Is it a closet where you store all your prayers?" That doesn't sound right. How could you do that?

"Well Kathleen, it is usually a quiet, secluded place where you can go and talk to God in private. It gives you personal interaction with God. No one is around to hear your innermost thoughts and conversations with Jesus."

The Bible says in Matthew 6:5-15, "Go into your room, close the door, and pray to your Father. He knows what you have need of before you ask."

Our God desires our prayers. He doesn't require fancy words or memorized phrases. He hears every single prayer. We can speak words in our own way and He understands us.

Sometimes it's hard to know what to say. Or how to say it. But don't be shy, God understands.

It's a time for us to read our Bible. That's how God talks to us. He reveals himself in His holy word. He teaches us right from wrong and how to live a happy life.

If we all lived by God's rules, this would be a perfect place.

"So where can we set up my prayer closet, Mom?" "We can find a small corner in your clothes closet. You can use that bean bag chair to sit in. I'll put a small table and lamp in there for your Bible and note book. It will be your special place, Kathleen, to talk to Jesus."

"Gee, Mom that sounds great. Thanks, let's go! Hurry. I need to talk to Jesus right now."

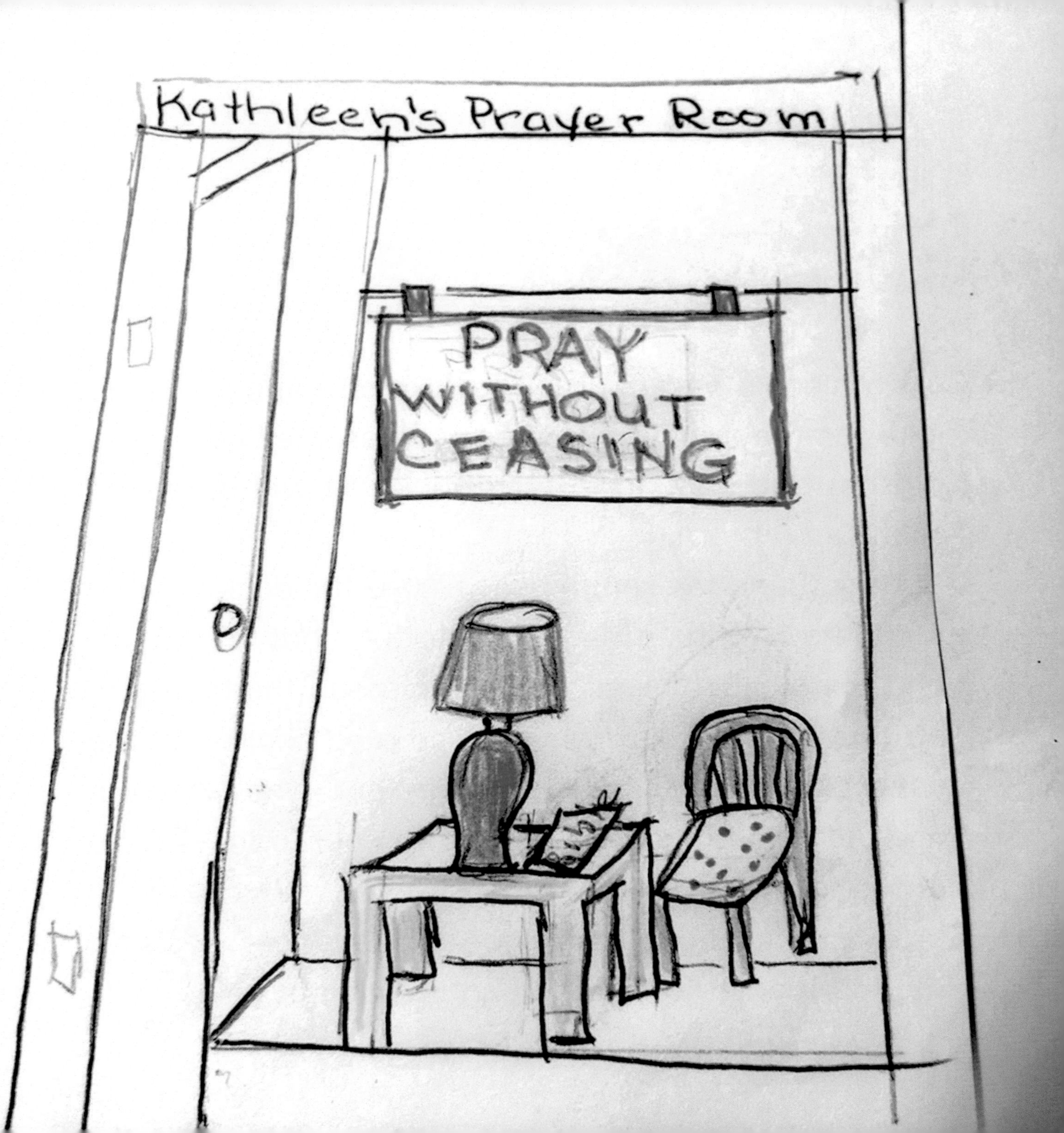

Kathleen's Prayer Room
PRAY WITHOUT CEASING

Mark 4:39

Kathleen's mom agreed to take all the girls to the lake for the day. It was breezy when they got there, but not bad enough to turn back. "It will die down soon" said mom.

They found the rental boat tied to the dock waiting for them. All the girls piled into the boat with mom and the picnic basket. Mom revved up the boat and off they went. The water seemed a bit choppy as the wind blew over the surface. The sun was hiding in and out behind the clouds. Halfway out to the middle of the lake, they began to worry.

"We better head back in!" said Misty. "Yes" said mom. "It's getting worse and it's kind of chilly too".

This reminds me of the scriptures in the Bible about the fierce wind that rocked the boat where Jesus was sleeping."

"Did it wake him up?" asked Wanda. "Did he get mad?" The disciples woke Him up all in a panic. They asked Him, "Do you not care that we are dying?"

He rose up in the boat and said to the wind, "Peace be still!" The wind ceased and everything was calm. He said to the disciples, "Don't you have faith?"

The disciples stared at each other in amazement. "Who can this be that even the wind and the sea obey Him?"

"It's getting even worse!" said Kathleen. "Let's hurry. We really need the faith to calm the waters. Wish Jesus was here to help us!"

"He is here!" said Misty. "We need much more faith than we have now! Our fear is holding us back."

By the time they got to the dock, the wind had died down a little. They were so glad to be on solid ground. "Thank you, Jesus!"

Genesis 3

"Just think how it would be if Adam and Eve didn't disobey God and eat the forbidden fruit from the Tree of Knowledge of Good and Evil. If only Eve didn't let that old "snake" talk her into disobeying God. Satan deceived Eve and she believed his lies.

Kathleen closed her eyes and tried to imagine how things might have been. I guess everyone would be naked, and not know it. Just like animals. They don't wear clothes because they don't realize they are naked.

We would have a beautiful garden to live in. All our food would be available without having to work at it. The weather would be perfect and lovely. There wouldn't be any pesticides because there wouldn't be any pests. We wouldn't have to work or do chores. That would be perfect.

We could talk to God, face to face. No disease or illnesses. "That's just too good to be true," said Pam. "I can't even imagine that!"

"What were the lies Satan told Eve?"

God told Eve that she would begin to die if she ate the forbidden fruit. Satan told her, "You will not surely die, but when you eat of it, your eyes will be opened and you will be like God."

God knew right away that they had eaten the forbidden fruit. They were hiding from God in the garden. God asked, "Where are you?" Of course, God knew where they were.

Adam said, "I heard your voice in the garden and I was afraid because I was naked and I hid myself." God asked, "Who told you that you were naked? Have you eaten from the tree of which I commanded you that you should not eat?"

The man said, "The woman whom You gave to me, she gave me of the tree and I ate it." The woman said, "The serpent deceived me and I ate."

Neither one wanted to take the blame for their actions. That serpent is very clever. Because of that God cursed us.

To the woman God said, "In pain you shall bear your children, your husband shall rule over you."

To the man Adam, He said, "The ground will be cursed and you will work hard to eat from it. Thorns and thistles will grow in it."

"Too bad!" said Kathleen. "We had it so good until Adam and Eve messed it up!"

But it was that Liar and Deceiver that led them astray.

Genesis 6-10

Kathleen was just waking up when she realized, "Today is Becky's birthday!" Her eyes flew open and she jumped out of bed. They had planned a big surprise party for Becky here at Kathleen's house.

"I hope Wanda remembers to bring the cake. She bakes such yummy cakes. Becky's favorite is chocolate cake with chocolate frosting. That's my favorite, too. We can put little plastic animals on top."

Becky is Kathleen's cousin. They got real close the summer they went to Bible camp together. Kathleen was excited to see her again. There was a real bond between those two. They always like to pray for each other. She and Kathleen had a close relationship. Kathleen was blessed with many good friends.

Pam was bringing snacks. She has so many good recipes. At 10 years, Pam was an accomplished cook.

As Kathleen and Misty were planning the party theme and decorations, it occurred to Kathleen to do a Noah's Ark theme. "It would be fun to use our stuffed animals as decorations."

"Hey Kathleen! What's the story about all those animals on a big boat? Did that really happen?"

"Yes! It did! You can read about it in the Bible. It's in Genesis 6-10."

God told Noah to build an ark. God gave Noah all the instructions and plans. He even specified the dimensions and what wood to use.

"What was the purpose?" asked Wanda.

"Well, God was very displeased with man and He was sorry He ever made man. He decided to destroy them all by a big flood."

"All of it? Everybody?"

"All but Noah and his family. He favored Noah."

"He chose male and female of every animal to keep the species alive on the face of the Earth. That's why the ark was so big."

"It rained 40 days and 40 nights until the whole Earth was covered with water. All the creatures on Earth died. It was almost a year before they were able to come out of the ark."

"When they came out of the ark, Noah built an altar and worshipped God. God was pleased. He promised He would never destroy the Earth by flood again. He set a rainbow in the sky as a sign of His promise."

"And that's why we have rainbows!", said Wanda. "I love rainbows!!! We must make some rainbows for the party!"

Noah's Ark

Matthew 19:14

    Misty and Kathleen were playing a Jenga puzzle. Kathleen had come to Misty's house to play a life size Jenga. It was getting as tall as Kathleen.

    Just as Misty was putting the last piece on the top, Jordan came running in the room at full speed. She had her arms outstretched and headed right for the Jenga Puzzle!!!!!

    Jordan was Misty's little 6-year-old sister. As the tower came crashing down, Misty yelled, "Mom!! Get her out of here!! She knocked down our tower and we were almost done. I was winning!"

    Jordan grinned a mischievous smile and said, "That's what you get for not letting me play with you."

Misty recalled the lesson that Mr. Garrett taught last Sunday about how Jesus loved the children.

Matthew 19:14 "Let the little children come unto me and forbid them not, for such is the Kingdom of Heaven."

Misty remarked, "Hope those children aren't like Jordan." She didn't really mean that, but she was upset with her little sister.

Kathleen asked, "Does that mean Heaven is full of kids?"

Matthew 18:3 "Unless you are converted and become as little children, you will, by no means enter the kingdom of Heaven."

"I think it means we must have the humble mind of a child and pure in heart.

Jesus loves the little children
All the children of the world
Red, yellow, black, and white
They are precious in His sight

Jesus loves the little children of the world.

"I guess we better be nice to her." Said Kathleen.

"We don't want Jesus to be mad at us."

Ephesians 6:11-18

"Hi," said Kathleen to the new boy in the Sunday School class. She wanted him to feel welcome and comfortable. She remembered how uncomfortable she was when she was new. Kathleen was always the one to greet the new kids.

He nodded his head her way, "I'm Ernie."

He was talking to Mr. Garrett. "I heard about the armor of God. What is that? Is it made of steel? That would be so cool."

"No", replied Mr. Garrett. "It's spiritual armor, but very effective against the powers of darkness and spiritual hosts of wickedness. For we do not wrestle against flesh and blood, but evil spiritual powers."

"Tell me about it." said Ernie eagerly.

The whole armor of God will enable you to withstand the wiles of the devil.

We must be strong in the Lord. Our conflicts are spiritual.

So, we need spiritual armor – God's armor.

"What are wiles?" asked Ernie.

"It's a trick intended to deceive and trap and to outwit." The devil doesn't want us to love and serve Jesus."

"We are to put on a waistband of truth. Jesus is the Way, the Truth and the Life! Satan is the father of lies and deception."

"Next, we wear a breastplate of righteousness. Righteousness is right standing with God."

"On our feet we place the Gospel of Jesus Christ."

"Then take up the shield of faith so we can defend ourselves from the fiery darts of the wicked one."

"I like the next one!" grinned Kathleen. "It's the helmet of salvation! This guards our minds against Satan's suggestions and lies."

"Don't forget the sword of the Spirit. That's the Word of God. Our Bible. We must always read it and follow its instructions."

The Word of God has power. It's a spiritual weapon we can use against Satan. Jesus used the Word of God against Satan when he tempted Jesus in the wilderness.

We need to always wear our armor of God. You never know when Satan is going to try to sneak into your life. God has given us this armor to be victorious over Satan's attacks and temptations.

Full Armor of God

Shield of Faith

Sword of the Spirit

Shoes of peace

Breastplate of Righteousness

Helmet of Salvation

Belt of Truth

Truth

Proverbs 3:5-6

"There sure are a lot of scriptures in the Bible about worry!" remarked Kathleen. "I guess we all worry too much. We must put our faith and trust in God."

"But that's so hard. Sometimes I just want to grab a problem by the horns and jump in to solve it. But that can lead to more problems and more worry," said Misty.

Proverbs 3:5-6 says, "Trust in the Lord with all your heart!"

"That's right!" agreed Misty. "We have a sign hanging on the wall that has that scripture written on it."

Kathleen added, "But there's more! The rest of the scripture says, 'Lean NOT on your own understanding.' What does that mean?"

"It means that you don't know everything and what you do believe, might just be wrong," Mom said.

"In verse 7, it says, 'Do not be wise in your own eyes.' That's the same thing. You think you know everything, but you certainly DO NOT!"

"In all your ways acknowledge Him, And He shall direct your paths."

"I want God leading me to the right path," said Misty. I think I would make too many mistakes without His guidance."

God's ways are not like our ways.

Further into Proverbs it says, "Wisdom is the principal thing; Therefore, get wisdom, and in all your getting, get understanding."

"Do not enter the path of the wicked, and do not walk in the ways of evil. Avoid it, do not travel on it; turn away from it and pass on."

"Gee", said Misty, "It sounds like God want us to be smart and not get into trouble. If we see a problem, we are to run the other way. Avoid the whole situation. That does take Wisdom."

"Heavenly Father, we want to follow God's ways. Help us to understand what those ways are. Give us wisdom to know the right path." Amen.

Exodus 20:1-17 Matthew 15:4 Ephesians 6:4

Kathleen found her mother in the kitchen preparing dinner.

"Mom? What does 'honor' mean?"

"Well, Kathleen, the dictionary defines "honor" as having respect for someone or something. You treat them special and lift them up."

"My Sunday school teacher, Mr. Garrett says we are to honor our father and mother."

"Yes," said Kathleen's mom, "that's one of the 10 Commandments that God gave us to live by. He even wrote them on tablets of stone and gave them to Moses."

"This is the first commandment that comes with a promise. If you honor your father and mother you will live a long life. But the Bible also says in Matthew 15:4 "If you curse your mother or father, you will be put to death."

"A commandment is something that is ordered by authority. It is a demand. It must be followed. God has reasons for His commandments. They are rules we should follow to make for a better life."

God knew that children and their parents would have problems with each other. He even instructed fathers not to provoke their children to anger. Ephesians 6:4

The Golden Rule follows right along with that;

"In everything, do unto others what you would have them do to you." Mathew 7:12

"You mean, even if that girl at school continues to treat me unkind, I have to be nice to her? I don't want to be nice to her especially when she calls me names." Stated Kathleen.

"I think that if you're really nice to her, she will turn around and be nice back." Said Mom

"We are all sinners. That makes us weak and unable to do what is right. That is why we all need Jesus.

How different our world would be if we all treated others the way we want to be treated."

John 15:2-6

The bright red geraniums were no longer bright. Kathleen's mom always had baskets of geraniums hanging in the backyard.

The days were getting colder and the flowers had turned brown and crispy. Kathleen's mom was removing the dead blossoms and trimming the brown leaves.

"Why do you do that, Mom?" asked Kathleen. "Doesn't that kill the plant?"

"Actually, it helps it to grow better and thicker. It gets rid of the dead flowers to make room for the new ones. The dead leaves are no longer useful."

When she was done, Kathleen walked up to look at the plant. It did look better.

"That's what God does for us," stated Kathleen's mom. "We are like the plant and the things in our life are the flowers and the leaves. God removes the useless things in our life, the things that hold us back from having a relationship with God."

"What things do you mean?"

"Things that hold us back from a productive, fullfilling life. Things like useless words and conversations, or bad attitudes or actions we should not do."

"God is life. He prunes off what is no longer vital and needed. Things that are dead and unhealthy so we can grow fresh! He's like the gardener that keeps all the plants trimmed and ready for new growth."

John 15:6 God said, "I am the vine and you are the branches. He who abides in me and I in him bears much fruit, for without Him we can do nothing."

John 15:5 "If anyone does not abide in Me, he is cast out and thrown into the fire."

We must be willing to allow God to prune out the dead stuff in our lives. Don't hang on to all that.

Matthew 14:13 Hebrews 11:1

Kathleen found her dad in his study. She asked him, "Dad, how can 5 loaves of bread and 2 fish feed 5000 men plus women and children? That's a lot of people and not very much food. How is that even possible?"

"With Jesus all things are possible!"

"He took the 5 loaves of bread and 2 fish, and looked up to heaven. He blessed them and broke them and gave them to the disciples to give to all the people.

"This is called a miracle. It's impossible for man to do it, but Jesus is God and He can do it."

"Dad! That would be awesome to be there and see that! Seeing is believing."

"But without seeing, and still believing, that is faith."

"I'm sure the people were amazed. A miracle causes people to believe."

"That would surely make me believe He was God."

"Jesus did many miracles during His ministry. He wanted people to know that He was God. God is alive and wants you to accept Him as Savior."

"Kathleen that brings to mind another scripture. It's the faith scripture."

Hebrews 11:1 "Now faith is the substance of things hoped for and the evidence of things not seen."

"I don't quite understand, Dad."

"It means you believe in something you cannot see. We believe in God even though we cannot see Him in the flesh. We have faith that He is."

"The people that Jesus was speaking to actually saw this miracle. They saw the bread and fish multiply before their eyes."

Jeremiah 29:11

Kathleen was happy to see her new friend, Marcie at Sunday School this morning. Ever since Kathleen met Marcie at the homeless camp, they had been friends.

Marcie spoke up in class to ask Mr. Garrett a question. The Bible says in Jeremiah 29:11 "For I know the plans I have for you", declares the Lord, "plans to prosper you and not to harm you, plans to give you hope and a future."

"Is that promise for me, too?", asked Marcie. It hasn't been pleasant to be homeless and live in a tent. Is that what God planned for me?"

"We never know what the future holds for us," said Mr. Garrett. "We change as our goals change. That promise is for all of us."

"Read verse 13, it will tell you, "You will seek me and find me when you seek me with all of your heart." He wants you to find Him."

"I have been praying and reading my Bible you gave me, Kathleen. In fact, my mom just got a job at the local Wal*Mart. She says we can start looking for a low-income apartment. That gives me hope!"

"Sounds to me that God is already working in your life to give you a future." said Kathleen. "Let's give Him praise!"

"For I know the plans
I have for you,"
declares the Lord,
"plans to prosper you
and not to harm you,
plans to give you
hope and a future.

Jeremiah 29:11

Malachi 3:8-10

Cliffy said to Kathleen, "Hey Sis! You are robbing from God!!" He noticed that she didn't have her tithes envelope when they left the house for church.

"What?" protested Kathleen. "In what way have I robbed God?"

"In tithes and offerings. The Bible says to bring our tithes and offerings to the storehouse."

"What storehouse?" questioned Kathleen.

"The storehouse of God, the church. We need to support our church. It takes lots of money to keep a church up and running. And we need to give our pastor a salary for all his work with us and the church.

He shouldn't have to get a second job to support his family."

"Verse 9 says, we are cursed because we robbed God. I don't want to be cursed. I want to be blessed."

Kathleen remembered this conversation because the next time they went to church, she had her little tithe envelope with her $2 in it. That was 10% of her allowance.

Pastor Jay happened to be preaching on tithes this morning. He said, "Tithing is proof that we are obedient to God. He will bless you. But we must give cheerfully. Don't complain or dread giving tithes and offerings."

In Malachi 3:10, God says "Test me and see if I don't throw open the flood gates of heaven and pour out so much blessing you cannot contain it."

Pastor Jay said that he tried to test God. He gave extra offering. The next week he got a raise at work. It doesn't always work so fast, but it shows us that God is true to His word.

Luke 1:28-31

Kathleen was climbing aboard the church bus with all her girlfriends. There was Wanda, Misty, Pam, Becky, Marcie, and a new girl named Gail. They were laughing and talking; so excited to be going to Church Camp.

The boys were going, too. Ernie loved camp and wouldn't miss it. Kathleen's brother, Cliffy was going along with Daniel, Keith, Billy, Scott, and William.

The camp was in the beautiful foothills of California. Mount Cross was a well-known campground for many churches. When they arrived, the boys and girls were separated into different dorms. Mr. Garrett was the counselor for the boys and Miss Olivia was the counselor for the girls.

But for now, they were all in the main meeting room. The counselors were discussing the plans for the week and the rules they were to follow:

Rule # 1 No boys in the girl's dorms, and no girls in the boy's dorms.

Rule # 2 You must clear your place at the table when you are done eating.

Rule # 3 Always bring your Bible, paper and pencil to the group meeting.

Rule # 4 Have fun.

It had been a busy, fun first day and the campers were getting tired. Time for bed and lights out.

The next day, each group met at their assigned study hall.

"Welcome girls," said Miss Olivia. "Today we are going to talk about a young girl from the Bible. She wasn't much older than you girls are. So, put yourself in her life and try to feel what she's going through."

"She was 12 or 13 years old and she loved God. She was an obedient child and found great favor with God. She prayed and talked with God every day. Her name was Mary."

"One day, an angel, named Gabriel came to her. He was sent by God. Gabriel told Mary that she was going to have a baby. This baby would be the Son of God."

"Mary was confused and a bit frightened. But she trusted in God. She was honored that God would choose her."

Mary wasn't married. The angel assured her that the baby would be put in her womb by God, The Holy Spirit.

"Now how would you feel?" asked Miss Olivia.

Gail, the new girl spoke up, "I would feel scared. Imagine an angel visiting you!!! I read that angels are very big and awesome, but very beautiful."

Wanda added, "It would be scary to find yourself with child and not married. That was not accepted."

"She was engaged to a man named Joseph", said Miss Olivia. "God had sent an angel to him as well to tell him about the baby. He knew it was God's Son and no one else."

"Any other man would think Mary was unfaithful to him."

Mary was moved and sang a song of praise to God. She was blessed to have been chosen to be the Mother of God.

At the same time Miss Olivia was teaching the girls about Mary and her baby-to-be, Mr. Garrett was telling the boys about Joseph, the man Mary was engaged to.

An angel appeared to Joseph in a dream saying, "Joseph, son of David, do not be afraid to take Mary as your wife for the baby she carries is of God, the Holy Spirit. And she will bring forth a Son and you shall call His name, Jesus."

Joseph went to the city of Bethlehem to register because he was in the linage of David. He took his betrothed wife with him. She was about to give birth.

Now Joseph was a special man. Imagine how you would feel when you discover your soon-to-be wife was already with child. It took a lot of faith to believe that she had not been unfaithful.

"I'll bet an angel of God could be pretty convincing, don't you?" said Ernie.

Mr. Garrett

Miss Olivia

I Thessalonians 4:13-18

Cliffy was in his bedroom practicing his trumpet. He had his bedroom door closed but we could still hear him. He sounded pretty good.

He was the bugle player for his Boy Scout troop. He knew all the bugle calls for every situation. He played the reveille which was the morning wake up call. There was the call to assembly, the call to mess (come eat) and taps (night). Kathleen got to hear her brother play for his troops when she and her parents went to Boy Scout camp with Cliffy last summer.

Kathleen was wondering what call Gabriel would play when God asks him to call His children home. Probably the call to assembly would be played.

I Thessalonians 4:13-18 tells us about the "Catching away" of those who are waiting and watching for Christ's return. The "dead in Christ" will rise first to meet Jesus in the air. Then those of us who are still alive will be caught up in the clouds to be with Him forever.

Kathleen asked," Does that mean we will fly up in the air?"

"That's what the Bible says!" stated Kathleen's mom. "It will be a wonderful experience. I think we will all be rejoicing and feeling God's love for us. But we have to be ready even though we don't know the day or the hour."

There will be those who are left behind. Those people who don't believe Jesus is our Lord and Savior and that He died for our sins. People who have turned away from God and rejected His Son.

Just then, Cliffy played his trumpet. He played the "call to assembly". This call signals troops to assemble at a certain place.

Maybe Jesus will come today and call us to meet Him in the air. What a glorious day that will be! I try to imagine what that will be like.

The Rapture

Cliffy playing his trump[

Becky

Wanda

Gail

marcie

Ernie

Pastor Jay

Pam

Misty

Jordan

Printed in the United States
By Bookmasters